proclaiming the living word

A HANDBOOK FOR PREACHERS

Gordon W. Lathrop

Augsburg Fortress

PROCLAIMING THE LIVING WORD
A Handbook for Preachers

Also available:
Love and Faithfulness: A Marriage Planning Handbook (ISBN 978-1-5064- 5060-5)
Remembering God's Promises: A Funeral Planning Handbook (ISBN 978-1-5064-3146-8)
Welcome One Another: A Handbook for Hospitality Ministers (ISBN 978-1-5064-1597-0)
Leading Worship Matters: A Sourcebook for Preparing Worship Leaders (ISBN 978-1-4514-7806-8)
Praying for the Whole World: A Handbook for Intercessors (ISBN 978-1-5064-1596-3)
Serving the Assembly's Worship: A Handbook for Assisting Ministers (ISBN 978-1-4514-7808-2)
Getting the Word Out: A Handbook for Readers (ISBN 978-1-4514-7807-5)
Altar Guild and Sacristy Handbook, 4th rev. ed. (ISBN 978-1-4514-7809-9)
Worship Matters: An Introduction to Worship (Participant book ISBN 978-1-4514-3605-1;
Leader guide ISBN 978-1-4514-3604-4)

Copyright © 2018 Augsburg Fortress. All rights reserved. Except for brief quotations in critical articles or reviews, no part of this book may be reproduced in any manner without prior written permission from the publisher. For more information, visit www.augsburgfortress.org/copyrights or write to: Permissions, Augsburg Fortress, Box 1209, Minneapolis, MN 55440-1209.

Scripture quotations, unless otherwise noted, are from the New Revised Standard Version Bible, © 1989 Division of Christian Education of the National Council of Churches of Christ in the United States of America. Used by permission. All rights reserved.

Cover design: Laurie Ingram
Cover photo: *Martin Luther's Sermon,* detail from a triptych, 1547 (oil on panel) (detail of 51406), Cranach, Lucas, the Elder (1472-1553) / Church of St. Marien, Wittenberg, Germany / Bridgeman Images
Interior design: Lauren Williamson
Editor: Jennifer Baker-Trinity

Manufactured in the U.S.A.

ISBN 978-1-5064-4789-6

20   19   18   17   16   1   2   3   4   5

Contents

Preface 7

Part I: Thinking about preaching 11
    Preaching in community
    Preaching the lectionary
    Central matters in every sermon
    What is preaching for?

Part II: Preparing to preach 43
    Study, attention, and imagination
        as tools
    Composing the sermon and giving it
    A schedule for the Sunday
        preacher's week
    A worksheet for sermon preparation

Conclusion 73

Further reading for the preacher 77

" We acclaim the living Word, Jesus Christ, present in the gospel reading. Preaching brings God's word of law and gospel into our time and place to awaken and nourish faith.

Evangelical Lutheran Worship,
"Pattern for Worship"[1]

Preface

This little book is intended as both a grateful encouragement and a concrete help for the Christian preacher. I hope that it might call the preacher again to courage, confidence, and even gladness in the task, and that it might enable refreshed reflection on what that task actually should be. At the same time, I am quite aware that preaching calls for humility and reverence before God and before the assembly of people gathered before God. It calls for even a certain amount of fear and trembling.

Augustine of Hippo, one of the greatest preachers in Christian history, said, "Insofar as I am a bishop"—that is, among other matters, a person responsible to speak the word of God in the assembly—"I am in danger." Preaching ought not be safe. It takes place before the resistance of the world and, at the same time, under the judgment of God. Still, with this book, I hope to call attention to the kind of risk the preacher appropriately takes, the kind of authority the preacher rightly claims, and to encourage preachers to know that they do not do their work alone. They do it in and for an assembly. They do it in a company of preachers. And sometimes, taking a break, they do not do it at all. Augustine added, "Insofar as I am a believer, I am safe." Preachers may better understand their own task by sometimes simply and gladly knowing that they cannot always do it and, instead, can take their place among all the believers, singing the communal song, listening to other readers and preachers, holding out their hands, too, for Christ in the holy communion, resting in the safety of the mercy of God, being sent with all the others toward our needy neighbors.

What follows is first, a consideration of what preaching is, then some thoughts about how to prepare, including one sketch of a possible schedule for the preparatory week, and a few suggestions about how actually to preach. The book concludes with a model worksheet for preparation and with a bibliography for further reading. Throughout, I hope the reader will feel accompanied, not least by the deep gratitude that Christian assemblies have for faithful preachers, a gratitude I share and want to embody here.

The title of the book includes two participles: *Proclaiming* and *Living*. Those participles follow, of course, from the reality that preaching is an event, an oral/aural communal occurrence within the flow of the communal and sacramental events that make up the Christian liturgy. This book, one of a series of Worship Matters Handbooks, seeks to consider the preaching event within that flow of events, as part of the flow, as one articulation of what it means that we have gathered in the name of the triune God around these texts, around word and sacrament together, and thus as interwoven with all else that happens in the assembly.

While I have sometimes taught preaching in seminaries, I am

not a homiletician. I have learned a great deal from homileticians, as I hope the bibliography included here testifies. But I am a pastor and preacher, a vocation I have exercised now for fifty years, and I am a liturgist who has tried to reflect on the relationship between critical biblical studies and Christian liturgical practice. It is thus as a preacher and a liturgist that I write about the importance and role of biblical preaching in Christian Sunday and festival assemblies. I also write as a Lutheran, imagining a Lutheran theological context and pointing to Lutheran resources. I nonetheless hope that these reflections may also be of use to Christian preachers who are not Lutheran, being received as one particular contribution to an important ecumenical discussion about preaching.

It may be that what you find here differs from how you have thought of preaching before or what you have learned in studying homiletics. If so, I hope that the differences become a stimulus for your own interior dialogue and a renewal—perhaps even a reformulation—of your own convictions and practice, whether you finally agree with what is written here.

In any case, I profoundly hope that you find yourself encouraged again toward faithful preaching. If you are a preacher, if you seek Sunday after Sunday to articulate law and gospel—our great need and God's far greater mercy in Christ—deep thanks to you for what you do.

Gordon W. Lathrop

Thinking about preaching

> Jesus Christ is the living and abiding Word of God. By the power of the Spirit, this very Word of God, which is Jesus Christ, is read in the Scriptures, proclaimed in preaching, announced in the forgiveness of sins, eaten and drunk in the Holy Communion, and encountered in the bodily presence of the Christian community. By the power of the Spirit active in Holy Baptism, this Word washes a people to be Christ's own Body in the world.
>
> *The Use of the Means of Grace*[2]

Preaching in community

The preacher is not alone. Indeed, preachers most certainly ought not consider themselves to be alone. That is the place for us to begin thinking about faithful preaching: in community. Of course, preachers must do much of the preparation work at their own desks, in their own minds, and drawing upon their own formation and educational resources. Of course, the preacher will expend personal energy in the task. Of course, the preacher must have courage to speak as a single voice in the assembly and to speak with appropriate authority, and such courage does sometimes feel like a lonely undertaking, especially when the speaking must necessarily be countercultural. But taking the further step of regarding preaching as a moment of individual self-expression, as a monologue in which the preacher talks about him- or herself or his or her views on things or focuses on his or her own experience, as the solitary adventure of the lone wolf or the singular religious entrepreneur, or as the agonized work of an existentially isolated thinker—such a step will inevitably, painfully mislead us.

There are strong counterweights to these misconceptions and significant counterstrategies to this loneliness. Consider these: The preacher rises to speak in an assembly of Christian believers; preaching is for that very assembly, and the assembly needs the preacher to do his or her work well. Indeed, many members of that assembly will be wishing the preacher well, praying for the preacher, even calling out to the preacher—silently or aloud—in support or in summons for the preacher to speak the gospel. It may be hoped that members of the assembly are engaging in an interior dialogue with the words the preacher speaks, a dialogue the preacher evokes. By congregational text study or simply by widely practiced congregational text reading in the week prior to the sermon, some assemblies regularize this support: many in the community have already been thinking about these texts and their meaning for the community before the preacher rises to preach from them. Sometimes they have been thinking aloud in pre-sermon conversation with the preacher. And sometimes—in an event many preachers receive as a great gift—the conversation will continue after the liturgy.

> Then the records of the apostles and the writings of the prophets are read for as long as there is time. When the reader has concluded, the presider in a discourse admonishes and invites us into the pattern of these beautiful things. Then we all stand together and offer prayer . . .
> *Justin, 1 Apology 67*[3]

More: preaching occurs as a moment in the communal liturgy, a part of the whole communal ritual process, integrated with all the events of the service:

- Before the sermon, the assembly has gathered, singing, and the preacher speaks in that singing community, articulating in spoken prose what the assembly has been singing about in the poetry of hymns and liturgical songs.
- The presider—the person who is most often the preacher—has greeted the assembly with the promised presence of the risen Lord, and the assembly has returned the greeting: "And also with you." The preacher needs to rely on that greeting and that promise, believing it gives what it says, knowing that the assembly thus also speaks the gospel to the preacher!
- A reader has read the biblical readings, a cantor or choir has led the assembly in singing the psalm, and the assembly has greeted the presence of the risen Christ in the gospel the preacher reads. The preacher's following words are then a further part of that communal encounter with the Word of God.
- After the sermon, in Lutheran practice, the congregation joins in the proclamation by singing a hymn of the day, usually followed by confessing the creed and always by praying for the needs of the world—needs that may well have been articulated in the sermon and needs that are held under the very promised mercy

of God that has been disclosed in faithful preaching. The sermon is integrated with these other forms of proclamation and prayer.

- Then the liturgy runs on to its second major event. The holy supper gives the communicant to eat and drink the very thing that the preacher has been responsible to give to everyone in words: Jesus Christ, his body and blood, for the life of the world.

Preaching thus ought not be a lonely, self-focused moment but a quite public engagement with the heart of these communal events, in the midst of the flow of these events and bringing their importance to expression.

> The proclamation of the word and the celebration of the sacraments are intimately connected. Preaching unfolds the significance of baptism and leads to the eucharistic table; both preaching and the sacraments are empowered by the word of God's promise.
> *Principles for Worship*[4]

More: the preacher is part of a company of preachers. Ordination welcomes one into the discipline of the church's preaching, in explicit partnership with others who bear this responsibility, and, along with those others, in vowed commitment to preach in accordance with the scriptures and with the creeds and confessions of the church. Anyone who is charged by the church with preaching joins this intentional, vowed company. That company may come into concrete expression for a preacher in various ways: in text study groups, in meetings of the ministerium, in online discussions, in reading the published counsel of other preachers, in the visitation of or conversations with one's bishop, simply in friendship and the exchange of ideas between preachers. It may also come to expression in the awareness that Christian preaching has been going on for a long time: it is wise for the preacher to know that she or he is working alongside Mary Magdalene, Paul, Polycarp, Perpetua, Augustine, Ambrose, Chrysostom, Dominic, Hildegard, Martin Luther, Henry Melchior Muhlenberg, Nicolai Grundtvig, Harriet Tubman, Dietrich Bonhoeffer, Martin Luther King, and many, many other nameless yet faithful articulators of the gospel of Jesus Christ. For some preachers, reading old sermons may become part of an important strategy to counter the lie of being alone. For all preachers, an awareness of the company of preachers and its vow should be a continually refreshing joy. This handbook on preaching means to be one small sign of that company.

In this regard, it should be noted that the Lutheran confessional concern that preachers should ordinarily be ordained ministers of word and sacrament is not an arbitrary or elitist rule. Ordination joins a person to this company of preachers, this common discipline. It also indicates that the preacher will have been thoroughly trained in biblical exegesis, liturgy, confessional and systematic theology, and pastoral care. Such formation is needed to enable responsible sermon preparation but also to equip the preacher for the individual pastoral conversations and group leadership that will inevitably arise if the preaching is profound. When, in cases of need, a layperson is authorized by the bishop for a temporary commitment to preaching, some replacements for that formation will need to be found: continuing education, pastors' conferences, serious reading, and distance learning—and perhaps even this little book—can all help existentially join the authorized layleader to the company of preachers. Laypeople who are asked to preach can find it immensely helpful to participate in this formation and find themselves accompanied, not alone.

And more yet: in our churches, the preacher preaches from the lectionary. Like Jesus in the Gospel according to Luke (see Luke 4:17), our preacher is *given* the texts. This ecclesial discipline places the preacher again in company—with the diverse biblical writers; with the people who worked to establish this lectionary; with the many, many assemblies throughout the world that are reading these texts on this day; with the churches in their continued commitment, manifest in the lectionary, to use the Bible not for just any purpose (and there are many ways the Bible can be used, not all of them salutary!), but for calling us again and again to faith in the God who is known in the gospel of Jesus Christ; and with the many other preachers called to work out this very purpose on this day. That is a remarkable company, one that makes for the end of both loneliness and lone-wolf adventures.

Preaching the lectionary

The lectionary is a disciplined ecclesial and ecumenical practice of reading the scriptures in local assemblies. As such, it provides one of the most important ways that the preacher is not alone. Preachers do not choose or own the texts for the day but receive them from the wider church, read them in common with the members of their own assemblies as well as with those of many other assemblies throughout the world, and join others of the company of preachers in the responsibility to bring those texts to expression today. *The Use of the Means of Grace* statement of the Evangelical Lutheran Church in America says such a lectionary "serves the unity of the Church, the hearing of the breadth of Scriptures, and the evangelical meaning of the church year" (7A). These purposes are not to be lightly dismissed. For further reflections on the origin, value, and structure of the Revised Common Lectionary (RCL)—the lectionary we will be considering here, the lectionary adopted by most North American Lutheran worship resources, and the lectionary marked by the widest ecumenical use throughout the world—see the suggestions in

"Further reading for the preacher" at the end of this book. Let me say the matter frankly: other currently available and individually created lectionaries are best avoided. They simply do not so clearly invite us into the wide ecumenical and ecclesial discipline of communally reading the rich fare of the Bible for the purpose of proclaiming Jesus Christ.

> The treasures of the Bible are to be opened up more lavishly, so that richer fare may be provided for the faithful at the table of God's word.
> *Constitution on the Sacred Liturgy*[5]

The RCL has another important value for us besides its ecumenical resonance: its brilliant structure corresponds to a profound pattern for preaching itself. Every set of lectionary readings is centered on the gospel reading of the day, anchored in a first reading that usually comes from one among the great variety of Old Testament sources, and supported by a second reading usually drawn from Paul, though also sometimes from one of the other New Testament letter writers. On this very model, the preacher is to center the sermon in the crucified and risen Christ, the One who comes to expression in the gospel and is symbolized by the gospel reading, and to do so while also using the images of the first reading to articulate the world's need and the mercy of God and using the images and exhortations of the second reading to propose that this encounter with Jesus Christ, with our need and God's mercy, is united with the message that was alive in the earliest Christian churches.

Thus, like the RCL, the sermon needs to attend to all three readings, serve the centrality of the gospel, bring to expression the meaning of the texts as they are read in a eucharist on Sunday or at a festival, and pay attention to current critical biblical studies.

There are three readings, and all three matter for the preacher. They are all three read into the event of the assembly, into the ears of the hearers. They are all three surrounded with acclamations by the assembly: The first is followed by a psalm, sung as a way in which the assembly reflects on and receives this reading from the Old Testament; the first and second readings are acclaimed as "The word of the Lord" or "Word of God, word of life"; and the gospel is received with praise to the risen Christ as the one actually present to the assembly in the reading. This serious, ritually intense reception of the readings matters for the preacher. The sermon will best be about these texts and about God in these texts, using these texts and their images to speak of Jesus Christ, of the world's need and God's mercy—to proclaim, thus, the living Word. While the sermon may focus especially on one of the three, all of them will be present in some sense: as the sermon, like the gospel reading, points to the presence of Jesus Christ; like the first reading anchors this proclamation in the ancient promises of God; and like the second reading surrounds what is said with the horizon of the church. Even a brief reference to the other readings—an image, a phrase—will help the preacher catch this purpose of the lectionary and will reassure the assembly that the preacher, too, has listened to all the readings that are still echoing in the room! To entirely ignore two of the readings is simply unwise. The church's lectionary sets out the readings of the day as a multi-plate feast; to eat from only one plate seems ungrateful, not to say unimaginative and narrow. The word of God is not a single idea; many voices in the Bible, in many different styles, bear witness to the mercy of God.

The "best reading" on any Sunday, however, is not necessarily the gospel. On a given Sunday or festival, the good news of God's mercy in Christ may come to its clearest expression in words from the Old Testament or from Paul. But, in the lectionary structure, the gospel is read as the capstone of the readings and is read after a gospel acclamation to the present Christ in order to demonstrate the church's hermeneutics: its principles for understanding the Bible in the assembly. The gospel book being read and the actual gospel text for the day are symbols of the crucified and risen Christ, and we read all the scriptures in such a way that this Christ is encountered and proclaimed through them. Whether the principal focus of the sermon is on the gospel text, the responsibility of the preacher is always to preach Christ. The gospel reading, its centrality, and its occurrence immediately before the preacher begins all symbolize that commitment.

The lectionary is made up of sets of readings from the Bible appointed to be read on Sundays and on the major festivals. As such, the lectionary brings to expression the purpose of

Sunday (and, for that matter, the purpose of such festivals as Christmas, Epiphany, Easter, and Pentecost): that in these texts and on this day the assembly gathers around the presence of the risen Christ and comes again to know the triune God, God as God is known in Jesus.

More: the lectionary texts are intended to be read at eucharist on Sunday: the same Spirit who enlivens the meal, the same Jesus Christ who gives himself away in this meal, and the same Father to whom we give thanks through Jesus Christ at the table—this triune God—is to be encountered also in these readings and in any sermon that seeks to understand these readings as words to us now. Paul says that the holy supper proclaims—preaches—the Lord's death until he comes (1 Cor. 11:26). Similarly, we may say that these lectionary readings are given to us for us to eat, like the scroll given to Ezekiel or to the elder John (see Ezek. 2:8–3:3 and Rev. 10:8-10). *Hearing* the word of the supper, we may also *eat* the contents of the scripture. Word and Meal interpret each other. Both lectionary and eucharist are full of "lamentation and mourning and woe" (Ezek. 2:10), the truth of the condition of the world. But they are also both full of the sweetness of the life-giving gospel (Ezek. 3:3; Rev. 10:11). The Spirit enlivens both word and meal. The crucified and risen Christ gives himself away in both. Preachers do well to listen to and consume them both, letting them then come to expression in their sermons, like both the prophet and the seer of the Apocalypse who then proclaimed what they had eaten.

The RCL takes the fourfold gospel of the New Testament quite seriously. So should the preacher. That theme from the best of current biblical studies was very important to the creation of this ecumenical lectionary. In the RCL, every year is marked by the dialogue between one of the synoptic gospels and the Gospel according to John: the synoptic "little apocalypse" and the synoptic account of the Baptist begin Advent, and the synoptic account of the baptism of Jesus is read on the first Sunday after Epiphany—but John is read on Christmas Day and on the second Sunday after Epiphany. The synoptic gospel of the year is then read in course through the year, with the synoptic passion account read on Passion Sunday; but John—especially in year A—determines the baptismal character of Lent and then—in all three years—provides the passion account for Good Friday and the Gospel for almost all of the Sundays of Easter. In year B, selections from Mark, the shortest of the synoptics, are supplemented with yet more of John. Similarly, the preacher should be aware of and able to speak about the different voices of the four books, neither collapsing them into a single story nor dealing with them as literal histories. The gospels—like the four living creatures of Revelation to which many Christians have compared them—are witnesses around and pointing to the Lamb. The preacher should join them. The witnesses are different, but they have a single purpose: one gospel in four voices.

Thus, the preacher should be able to bring to expression the uniqueness of each gospel's understanding of Jesus: the presence of the hidden Messiah in Mark; the new law-giver in Matthew; the table-host who serves in Luke; and the incarnate judgment and grace of the Word in John.

That seriousness about the fourfold gospel also implies another important result from critical biblical studies that matters to the lectionary and should form the preacher: every pericope, every portion-text from a gospel, stands for the whole book. Any narrative in one of the canonical gospels can be seen as leaning forward to the culminating narrative of the death and resurrection of Jesus and to his presence in the assembly now. Biblical studies have come to see that the gospels are narratives of Jesus' presence now. As Luther wrote in "A Brief Instruction on What to Look for and Expect in the Gospels," a story of Christ healing or forgiving should be heard as witnessing to the Crucified and Risen One coming here, and here now, forgiving and healing us. In preaching, the themes of the great feasts ought to be expressed similarly. The Child of Christmas, for example, is always also the incarnate Word and the one who goes to the cross and the Risen One present in the assembly. All together. Each feast—exactly like each gospel pericope—is seen as one facet of the single, brilliant jewel that is the good news of God. The preacher invites us to look at the whole jewel through this facet.

> When you open the book containing the gospels and read or hear how Christ comes here or there, or how someone is brought to him, you should therein

> perceive the sermon or the gospel through which he is coming to you, or you are being brought to him. For the preaching of the gospel is nothing else than Christ coming to us, or we being brought to him. When you see how he works, however, and how he helps everyone to whom he comes or who is brought to him, then rest assured that faith is accomplishing this in you and that he is offering your soul exactly the same sort of help and favor through the gospel. If you pause here and let him do you good, that is, if you believe that he benefits and helps you, then you really have it. Then Christ is yours, presented to you as a gift. After that it is necessary that you turn this into an example and deal with your neighbor in the very same way, be given also to him as a gift and an example.
>
> Martin Luther, *What to Look for and Expect in the Gospels*[6]

The lectionary also takes the polyphony of the Old Testament, its many voices and many stories, quite seriously. The very diversity of kinds of literature in these scriptures enriches the feast of reading in the liturgy. While that diversity is treasured, however, the discoverable common theme of the Old Testament's many books again and again underlines both human failure and God's promise. Christians use that theme—and the actual narratives and images of the Hebrew scriptures—to speak about what has happened and is happening in Christ. The preacher should be prepared to have his or her speech enriched by Old Testament images and anchored in the biblical themes of failure and promise, sin and forgiveness, death and life.

It is important for a preacher to note that during half of the year the RCL provides two options for the first reading. Lutheran preachers need to be aware that the second of these choices (as listed in pages 38–53 of the "Propers" section of *Evangelical Lutheran Worship*)—the so-called "semicontinuous reading"—was developed largely for the use of churches with a preaching hermeneutic different from the one suggested here, centered instead on teaching a version of biblical history. In the RCL, the first reading throughout the year—including the first, or complementary, option for the first reading on the standard Sundays between Trinity Sunday and Christ the King—has been chosen in intentional dialogue with the gospel pericope, its imagery or its narrative mattering immensely for the gospel. It may often be regarded as the scripture on which the gospel functions as a sermon. The whole set of texts then has an intention: to proclaim Jesus Christ now. With the semicontinuous readings, that intention remains less clear and more difficult to bring to expression. While Lutherans can rejoice at sharing the RCL with many other Christians, for the life of their own congregations the complementary reading will almost always be a wiser choice.

Sometimes, of course, there will be preaching on weekdays. Lenten and Advent midweek services provide ready examples. There is an ecumenical Daily Lectionary (see pages 1121–53 of

Evangelical Lutheran Worship), but it is not really a preaching lectionary. It is rather a set of texts that support and echo the Sunday readings, usable in family life and communal services of daily prayer. My recommendation is that midweek preaching will do better to use some or all of the very Sunday readings that the Daily Lectionary is meant to recall or anticipate. If the midweek sermon is not using a series of texts chosen locally, another sermon that reflects on one or more of the Sunday readings can be wonderful. There is enough in any set of lectionary readings for many sermons!

The lectionary, thus, makes a proposal about preaching. A sermon should do what the gospel book does, using the imagery of that book, juxtaposed to the images of the Hebrew scriptures and the witness of Paul or one of the later New Testament writers. Such a sermon is not a Bible study, not an attempt at imagining what it might have been like at a time other than now. It is rather a means of the presence of Christ, the living Word of God, now, in this assembly. It is a communal meal in words. It should articulate "lamentation and mourning and woe" and yet offer the taste of the gift of Christ that restores life. Such a sermon offers an encounter with the mystery of God at the heart of the scriptures and a means of communal participation in that mystery.

Central matters in every sermon

This combination of articulating the condition of need in the world and articulating the life-giving presence of Christ is called "preaching law and gospel." Every faithful sermon should be marked clearly by this pair in this order. What is meant here is not an artificial creation of a problem by the preacher that the preacher then solves. Nor is such preaching to be a manipulation of people's emotions, first sadness and then joy, though profound emotion may indeed freely follow upon honest speech by the preacher. Nor is the preacher the judge, since he or she also stands under the judgment of God articulated in the scripture. Nor is the preacher personally the good news, though she or he is indeed meant to speak and give that good news directly to the hearers. Rather, the preacher is simply to tell the truth about our awful sin, failure, and death, and about God's stunning gift.

> Preaching is the living and contemporary voice of one who interprets in all the Scriptures the things concerning Jesus Christ. In fidelity to the readings appointed for the day, the preacher proclaims our need of God's

> grace and freely offers that grace, equipping the community for mission and service in daily life.
> *The Use of the Means of Grace*[7]

The truth of the law should be so articulated that we recognize our situation, honestly described, though most likely described with a directness rarely encountered in our world of circumlocutions for death (so often, in common speech, we "pass" or even "transition;" we do not die) and nice speech that avoids our actual failures. In preaching the law, the actual situation of the current world needs to be addressed. Honesty about our need, sin, and death, and honesty about God's judgment: such is preaching the law. Indeed, without reference to the real burdens and sorrows, political failures, and social sin that oppress our world, the speech of a sermon may too easily seem as if it is simply a fairy tale, spun out in a world quite other than the one we know.

Then the truth of the gospel should be so articulated that we find ourselves invited to trust it with our lives and so discover ourselves awakened to hope and faith. The preacher ought to actually forgive with the forgiveness of God, actually speak the presence of Christ, actually pour out the life-giving Spirit in words. This forgiving, this speaking, and this outpouring constitute the genuine authority of preaching. We have no other.

The preacher finds the primary resource for these articulations of law and gospel—death and life, need and mercy, sin and forgiveness—in the imagery of the readings for the day, thus in one or more of the repeated biblical accounts of human failure, God's judgment, and God's renewing mercy. Law and gospel are both in the Old Testament, filling its stories with judgment and hope. And they are both in the New Testament. But, for Christians, the deepest truth of this judgment and mercy is found in Jesus Christ, his ministry, his cross, and his resurrection, and thus the capstone of the readings and their interpretive key is found in the gospel reading of the day.

Law and gospel should mark every sermon. As the preacher prepares, she or he will want to reflect on recent experiences with people in need as well as on what can be learned from good journalism—a reliable newspaper or reliable online news sources, for example—or from good art—a novel, for example. Human duplicity and selfishness, warfare and torture, prejudice and addictions, the misuse of the earth and of each other: all these will come to mind. But then the preacher will look for images that bear the biblical pattern of law and gospel in each of the texts. At the heart of this search will once again be the discovery of mercy: God in Christ takes on our death and sin and, against any expectation, makes of this death the very place where abundant life flows. That is the life-giving gospel. When the sermon is ready, the preacher will want to check that she or he is indeed prepared to honestly speak of our need and God's mercy in Christ, ready to preach law and gospel here, now, in this assembly. You, dear preacher, know that preaching is that serious.

But there are also other central matters that should be present in every—or nearly every—sermon. Here is a list:

As Paul counsels, the sermon will speak the cross of Christ (1 Cor. 1:23; 2:2). Here are some questions to use in preparation: Using the terms of these texts, how has God saved the world in the death and resurrection of Jesus? What is the atonement as it is imaged in these readings? How does this particular gospel reading lean forward to the passion and resurrection account in the gospel book in which it figures? Then, how might the images in the first reading be borrowed or reborn to speak of what God has done in the cross and in the Risen One coming here, now? Asking these questions urges the preacher to make sure that what God has done in Jesus Christ—and not simply any "good news"—makes up the heart of the sermon. Like the image of Luther preaching on the cover of this book, the preacher finds in every biblical text the grounds for pointing the gathered assembly toward the cross. And, following the indication of the blowing loincloth in that same image, this Crucified One lives in the resurrection, providing for us the very source of the life-giving Spirit of God, the wind of God that breathes our bones to life.

> I decided to know nothing among you except Jesus Christ, and him crucified.
> 1 Corinthians 2:2

More: the assembly that hears the reading of the day has

gathered for eucharist. It has also gathered by remembering baptism and sometimes welcoming a new Christian to the community through baptism. The sermon should articulate, however briefly, the meaning of baptism and of the supper. How is the gospel that the sermon will proclaim the very word that is poured over us in baptism, the word that we come back to again and again as baptism marks our daily life? How are these texts today words that, with the water, make up the promise of baptism? To say the matter in one way, does hearing these texts proclaimed put us to death and raise us to life with Christ, as in Paul's understanding of baptism? And how do we eat and drink this gospel in the holy communion? How can we invite our hearers to receive the very content of these texts when they receive the presence of Christ in the eucharist? Asking such questions provides the preacher with a means to test the seriousness and sacramental depth of the sermon.

And the Trinity: we have been gathered together in "the grace of our Lord Jesus Christ, the love of God, and the communion of the Holy Spirit" (2 Cor. 13:13). In the midst of this gathering, how does the Trinity come to expression in the sermon? In the terms of these texts, can it be seen that the Spirit gathers us into Jesus Christ to stand in him before the One who sent him and to turn with him toward the needs of our neighbors? Asking such questions calls us to see that our preaching is really about the God of the church's confession, not about currently popular cultural ideas of divinity. Not only *about* this God, our preaching is to gather us *into* the Trinity: according to the fourth gospel, the Spirit enlivens the word from Jesus (John 14:26), and the Father and the Son make their home where that word is kept (John 14:23). Or, as Luke says (4:16-30), the sermon takes a text juxtaposed to yet other texts and, in the power of the Spirit and fulfilling these texts in our hearing, Jesus Christ becomes the today of God, a today full of both judgment and promise. We proclaim the living Word.

> Jesus answered him, "Those who love me will keep my word, and my Father will love them, and we will come to them and make our home with them . . . the Advocate, the Holy Spirit, whom the Father will send in my name, will teach you everything, and remind you of all that I have said to you."
> John 14:23, 26

Other matters may appear in the sermon from time to time. A particular moment in the liturgy may come into special focus because of the texts of the day: thus, when Isaiah 6 is read on Trinity Sunday in year B or the fifth Sunday after Epiphany in year C, the "Holy, Holy, Holy" of the great thanksgiving may be discussed (and the bread and cup of communion may be seen as Isaiah's burning coal!). The meaning of the peace in the liturgy may become clear in a sermon on the texts of the second Sunday of Easter in all three years, when John 20:19-31 is read of the risen Christ giving peace to the Sunday assembly. Or the seasons of the church year will need to have some effect. The accent of Advent on the world waiting for justice, the accent of the Sundays after Epiphany on mission, the accent of Lent on baptismal renewal, and the accent of the Sundays of Easter on the meaning of the resurrection all come to expression in the lectionary readings and should also come to expression in preaching. Or commemorations of faithful Christians of the past may be occurring near the time or on the day of the sermon. Those Christians may provide examples of what faith looks like when it becomes the source of a life, and a sermon may sometimes utilize that example as it calls us again to faith and so to faith active in love. Or a disaster or a national holiday or an event in the life of the congregation may require a comment integrated into the focused proclamation of law and gospel. Or a hymn that is sung may provide a stanza or a phrase that coincides wonderfully with the articulation of the gospel on this day. Or a hymn may require some explanation, in the light of the texts of the day, so as to avoid it being misunderstood.

These matters may sometimes occur in preaching. And preaching itself may vary in length and style, structure and imagery—just as the gospels and the narratives of the Old Testament vary. But law and gospel, the cross and resurrection of Jesus Christ, the sacraments—or at least one of them—and the Trinity should always be there. Always.

Why?

Because of the purpose of preaching.

Sometimes, in the life of the churches, there is a fair amount of confusion about this purpose. One author speaks about "pulpits without purpose" (see the book by C. J. LaRue listed in "Further reading for the preacher"). Popularly, preaching comes across as simply one person telling other people what to do; maybe even that one person is yelling at other people about what they should do or not do. I hope not. But even where preaching makes a positive impression, people may still imagine that preaching is one person talking about his or her ideas about religion, perhaps using his or her personal experience as primary resource, so that we, too, might think about religion and our experience. It will be clear from what has been said here so far that I think this an inadequate definition.

What is preaching for?

Then what *is* preaching for?

The Augsburg Confession, the basic confessional text of the Reformation churches and an important sixteenth-century appeal for unity among all the churches, has an answer for us. According to the Confession, preaching—like the sacraments—has a purpose: to be the means through which the Holy Spirit is given so that we might come to faith. In Article V, which the German text titles *Vom Predigtamt,* "Concerning the Office of Preaching," the Confession defines "the means of grace," the ways God gives the Holy Spirit to us so that we might be brought to faith. Those ways—those means—include especially the preaching of the gospel and the giving of the sacraments. The Article, which immediately follows the discussion of justification, says that we cannot receive forgiveness of sin and become righteous before God by our own works but only by grace given for Christ's sake through faith, when we believe what God has done in Christ to bring us to life. The Confession then continues:

> To obtain such faith God instituted the office of preaching, giving the gospel and the sacraments. Through these, as through means, he gives the Holy Spirit who produces faith, where and when he wills, in those who hear the gospel.[8]

The Latin text of the same Article, now titled *De ministerio ecclesiastico*, "Concerning Ministry in the Church," says it this way:

> So that we may obtain this faith, the ministry of teaching the gospel and administering the sacraments was instituted. For through the Word and the sacraments as through instruments the Holy Spirit is given, who effects faith when and where it pleases God in those who hear the gospel . . .[9]

What is preaching for? To bring us again and again to faith, to trusting God, to believing that what God has done in Christ gives us and all the world forgiveness, hope, and life. Preaching is intended to awaken faith in all its hearers, the new believer just learning to trust God as well as the veteran Christian who also needs always to learn that trust again. Such faith is not simply some general human trust that things will get better. Rather, it is the specific reliance on what God has done in Christ, engendered by the Holy Spirit working through law and gospel and through the proclamation of the cross. Furthermore, when genuine, such faith inevitably turns with Christ toward the needs of others, becomes "faith working through love," as Paul says in Galatians 5:6. Trusting that God in Christ has freed us from the fear of death and of judgment—that Christ has taken our wretchedness and given us his blessedness (so Luther in the 1519 essay on "The Blessed Sacrament of the Holy and True Body of Christ")—Christians rightly turn toward the wretchedness of others, wanting themselves to be signs of life and hope for our neighbors in the needy world. Preaching rightly makes that outgoing shape of faith clear.

This purpose for preaching also comes to expression by the location of the sermon in the liturgy. The sermon follows and thus is responsible to the lectionary texts that have been read. Then, after the sermon, the assembly expresses the faith God awakens in us through the living Word, by proclaiming this faith in the hymn of day or in the words of one of the ancient creeds or both. The assembly also expresses its trust in God—the God whose promises both the scriptural texts and the sermon have proclaimed—by praying for all the needy world, believing that God hears such prayer. We then turn to receiving Christ in the eucharist, the meal meant to strengthen our faith. And so strengthened, we are sent, so that faith might indeed be active in love for our neighbors.

The preacher then asks himself or herself: Does my sermon tell the truth about our need and God's mercy? Does it give forgiveness, bear witness to the presence of Christ, pour out the Spirit? Using these texts, in all their varied though united images, and speaking anew of the cross, the sacraments, the holy Trinity, in the terms of these images—indeed *speaking the very presence of the Crucified and of the holy Trinity,* proclaiming thus the living Word—does my sermon invite to faith and so to faith active in love?

There is deep joy, a constant recovery of our vocation, and yet continued challenge for the preacher who discovers this clear purpose for his or her preaching. And both that joy and that challenge will affect how the preacher prepares.

> It is also taught that at all times there must be and remain one holy Christian church. It is the assembly of all believers among whom the gospel is purely preached and the holy sacraments are administered according to the gospel.
>
> *Augsburg Confession*[10]

Preparing to preach

> O mortal, eat what is offered to you, eat this scroll, and go, speak to the house of Israel.
>
> Ezekiel 3:1

Study, attention, and imagination as tools

For all of the disciplined communal character of preaching, we come now again to the pastor's desk and the preacher's individual work. Preaching does require such work. I have thought that this preparatory work of the preacher might be summed up as "study, attention, and imagination." Let me be clearer.

A preacher begins to prepare, of course, by reading the texts appointed in the lectionary for the Sunday or festival liturgy as part of which the sermon will occur. First, he or she simply reads them, paying attention. I like to do this at least a week before the event itself. I begin with the gospel text, then turn to the other texts, on the grounds that the gospel always provides the symbolic center for what the preacher must finally do in preaching. But I carefully read the other texts as well, attending especially to their images and their patterns of failure yet promise, death yet life. I make a simple outline of each text, noting important phrases and verbal images. In this initial reading it is important not to skip any part that is puzzling or hard, any part that remains unsolved in a first reading—what some people call an *aporia*, a surprising contradiction or paradox in the text. As these readings work in the memory of the preacher in this coming week, it may very well be that the difficult and unsolved parts give the greatest gifts in the end.

In any case, study begins with simply and carefully reading the texts. The intention here is to make these readings available to the preacher's memory as she or he goes about ordinary life and the ordinary work of ministry in the coming week, trusting that possibilities for preaching will arise from the juxtaposition of the texts with events in life and ministry.

On a subsequent day, sitting at a desk or in a good place for reading, this study can continue and deepen. If the preacher knows the biblical languages, she or he can read the texts now in the Greek and Hebrew or Aramaic. The rewards of this practice are manifold. One gift is the encounter with the rich vocabulary of the texts, a vocabulary depth not always caught by the English translation. Another gift is simply that such reading will, for most people, need to be slower and more attentive than reading in English. Such slower reading may bring along a necessary distancing from the texts, a new encounter with their strangeness and their surprises. Biblical stories or sayings are sometimes known too well, domesticated, harmonized, remembered in a children's Bible version. Reading slowly in the original language can help reveal again the particularity—even the difficulty—of the actual text. This latter possibility may also be at least partly available to people who have no capability in the biblical languages if they read the texts in another language that they do know. That, too, may enable reading slowly. Yet another exercise might be to read the texts in several different reliable English translations.

Then the study needs to go on, perhaps on yet another day or perhaps right then. One next step should be to read the context of each text in the biblical book in which it appears. Ongoing, regular reading by the preacher, part of his or her ordinary study not directly related to immediate sermon preparation, should have helped him or her know the characteristics of each of the gospels, something about Paul's work, and a basic awareness of the prophets, the Psalms and the wisdom literature, and the structure and sources of the history books and the Torah. Now this knowledge will help the preacher think about the context of the lectionary's texts. The point is not that the sermon will be public Bible study but that Christian proclamation must use the texts honestly and maturely. One helpful practice might be to carefully read the whole of one of the synoptic gospels at the outset of the lectionary year when that gospel figures largely—and to regularly read the whole of the Gospel according to John every year.

Then a preacher will be helped by knowing the intertextual references used in the day's texts: What passages from the Old Testament are being quoted or alluded to in the gospel or in Paul? How does the gospel pericope of the day differ from the ways in which the other gospels use the same event or the same discourse? Those differences can again help the preacher to attend to *this* gospel text. Assistance in finding these intertextual references is available. A synopsis of the four gospels will make the parallel passages clear. Footnotes or marginal notes in some study Bibles will do the same. Those study Bibles may also help with the Old Testament sources that the Christian writings have used. If the preacher reads the New Testament in Greek, the Nestle-Aland edition has splendid marginal notes that make the gospel parallels and almost all of the intertextual references clear—another gift that comes from reading the Greek—and the boldface type indicates actual Old Testament quotations. Checking words in a comprehensive lexicon can also lead to other passages where the same word or sequence of words occurs.

This study of intertextuality is important because a knowledge of the rebirth or reuse of Old Testament imagery for the purposes of the gospel book or of other New Testament writings is one of the great sources for preachers who wish to join the classic Christian use of the scriptures in their proclamation. How does the New Testament writer use the old scriptures to preach Christ? Then, awareness of the particular witness of one gospel book as compared with the others provides another such source. Perhaps the most important question for the preacher will be this: How does this gospel writer use this particular passage to point toward the cross and resurrection of Jesus at the end of the gospel book and toward the continued presence of the Risen One in the assembly of the church now?

An important next step in study will be careful consideration of the images used in this set of texts. Sources for this study include the yearly Augsburg Fortress online publication *Sundays and Seasons*, with its repeated section "Images in the Readings," and the 2002 Fortress Press book, *Treasures Old and New: Images in the Lectionary* (see "Further reading for the preacher" on page 77), with its lectionary-keyed indexes. It may very well be that one or more of the images alive in these texts will provide the preacher the best way to speak of our need and God's mercy in Christ on this Sunday, to articulate the life-giving presence of Christ toward which the gospel text in juxtaposition to both of the other readings points.

> My God, my God, thou art a direct God, . . . that wouldst be understood literally and according to the plain sense of all that thou sayest. But thou art also . . . a figurative, a metaphorical God too: a God in whose words there is such a height of figures, such voyages, such peregrinations to fetch remote and precious metaphors, such extensions, such spreadings, such curtains of allegories, such third heavens of hyperboles, so harmonious elocutions . . . ; thou art the dove that flies.
> John Donne, *Devotions Upon Emergent Occasions*[11]

Only then will it be time for the preacher to turn to the commentaries. Perhaps she or he has a one-volume commentary that has been especially reliable. Perhaps, over the years, a little library of brilliant commentaries from different series has been accumulated: Raymond Brown or C. H. Dodd on John, for example, or Adela Y. Collins on Mark, or Walter Brueggemann on Isaiah. Such a discriminating collection is a wise idea. In any case, reading in the commentaries can deepen what the preacher has found already, propose ideas that have not yet been considered, and begin to propose some solutions for the parts of the texts that remain a puzzle, while possibly deepening the puzzle elsewhere.

Two other matters belong to preparatory study. First, the preacher should think about the ways these texts will echo within this particular liturgy. Help can be found in the other proper texts of the day: the prayer of the day and the other short prayers; the psalm; the hymns that will be used, including especially the hymn of the day; the gospel acclamation; the proper preface; the particular thanksgiving at the table that will be used; and the commemorations that will occur in the week prior to or following the Sunday. Do any of these provide connections that express the meaning of the texts and that should be present, however briefly, in the sermon? The prayer of the day in *Evangelical Lutheran Worship,* for example, has often been crafted to draw the assembly into standing before God in the readings that follow and can also, thus, contribute to the focus of the preacher, who hopes to do the very same thing. In addition, the preacher might plan to turn some attention toward the hymn of the day that will immediately follow the preaching, so that the hymn is opened (the biblical references and the original social context of some hymns do need opening!) and sermon and hymn work together in the mouth and mind of the assembly. Help for choosing the hymn of the day—and for choosing the hymns generally—can be found in several places, including especially *Indexes to Evangelical Lutheran Worship* (Augsburg Fortress, 2007). Help with the origin and the original meanings of the hymns, information that may be helpful to briefly mention in preaching, can be found, among other places, in the *Hymnal Companion* by Paul Westermeyer (Augsburg Fortress, 2010). Then what other connections to the liturgy might there be? (For one response, see *Sundays and Seasons,* "Connections to the Liturgy.") What is the season of the church year, for example? How do the texts help us see the whole gospel through the facet of this season? More: as ideas for the sermon begin to develop, can the preacher especially consider how to invite the assembly to eat and drink in holy communion the very gospel that is being proclaimed in the preaching? How do these texts relate to communion?

Second, the preacher may want to consult lectionary-based preaching resources (*Sundays and Seasons: Preaching* provides one of many), collections of sermons, or historical examples of other preachers working with these texts. For some suggestions on finding such classic sermons, see "Further reading" on page 77. *Sundays and Seasons* provides specific help in the integration of all three texts. In addition, pages 140-42 of *Saving Images* sets out two examples.

All of this study will not yet yield a sermon. What it will give is some material from which a sermon may be made. In order to proceed to the making, that material will need to be surrounded with a context that helps the preacher take the next steps toward having a sermon ready for the liturgy. Part of that context will involve a return from solitary study to the community in which preaching occurs. One way such a return can occur is by the preacher's participation in communal discussion of the texts: local study groups with other preachers, parish text study occasions, individual conversations with parish members or other preachers.

But whether the preacher has the gift of such communal conversations, two further matters will need to surround the preacher's study: attention and imagination. By *attention,* I mean the practice of listening and focusing and yielding that has already been active in the preacher's reading of the texts. Indeed, one of the core reasons why careful reading of the texts is so important—one of the further gifts, for example, of reading in original languages—is that it involves practice in paying attention. But the preacher will need to turn this same focus toward the assembly he or she serves and toward the world in which the sermon will occur. Before speaking, the preacher needs to listen and look. Such listening and looking involves a certain bracketing of the self, even a kind of humility. Me and my opinion are not the only things that matter. I need to attend to the mystery of each person I meet, each person who may gather in the Sunday assembly, and I need to attend to the mystery of the assembly itself, its identity and purpose in the triune God. I need to attend to the mystery of the world, its manifold and pluriform wretchedness and blessedness.

In exercising this attention, *imagination* will be important. Imagination has helped me consider the surprising meaning of the texts. It will also help me consider how other people may be surprising or even strange, what the human condition may be, how most people carry deep, hidden hurts or longings. It will also make my world larger. Imagination can consider other cultures, other ways people pass life on to their children, that are alive in this and in other places. It can similarly consider the situation of other species of life that inhabit God's good world. And it can let me inhabit at least a little of the sorrow with which the world is everywhere so full.

> They wandered in the valley forever; and they smote the rock, forever; and the waters sprang, perpetually, in the perpetual desert. They cried unto the Lord forever, and lifted up their eyes forever, they were cast down forever, and He lifted them up forever. No, the fire could not hurt them, and yes, the lion's jaws were stopped; the serpent was not their master, the grave was not their resting-place . . . Job bore them witness, and Abraham was their father . . . Shadrach, Meshach, and Abednego had gone before them into the fire,

> their grief had been sung by David, and Jeremiah had wept for them. And they looked unto Jesus, the author and finisher of their faith . . .
> *My soul! don't you be uneasy!*
> James Baldwin, *Go Tell It on the Mountain*[12]

A preacher's daily life and ordinary ministry should be already full of occasions for attention and imagination. Parish meetings and pastoral conversations, parish visitation and preparation for and participation in weddings, births, and funerals all provide such occasions to pay attention. The human experiences the preacher observes, the joys and sorrows, the flow of daily life, the topics of concern, the preacher's own experiences—all matter intensely.

> Life in the Christian community is a gift that forms and nourishes the ministry of preaching. . . . Those who preach are formed by the communities in which they serve. They stand in the midst of the people in joy and in sorrow, receiving as well as giving comfort and admonition. They are strengthened in knowing that they do not have all the words, nor could they, but that they serve in partnership with Christ and the whole people of God.
> *Principles for Worship*[13]

But the quiet people in the assembly, the people who sit in the back row and never make appointments with the pastor, also need to be listened to. Their situation also needs to be imagined. And much more: the preacher ought regularly read a reliable newspaper or news source or two, not simply news filtered through social media or unreliable broadcasting. Indeed, the preacher should read novels or poetry that help with the imagination of the human situation and make the gift of eloquent and accurate language (like the astonishing language of James Baldwin), thus broadening the linguistic tools of the preacher; history that describes the development of our communities and surprising truths about our pasts; science that probes the actual circumstances of the things that are. And more yet: the preacher should be paying attention to the natural and social environment where she or he lives. Where does the water come from and what is its condition? What is happening with the weather and the land? Is good food available to everyone? Are protection and social services and fair policing similarly available? What other species live here and how are they? What is beautiful, alive, healthy? What degraded?

I do not mean to say that preaching should be a report on what my attention has seen or a telling of imaginative stories that I have read or that I have made up. For one thing, there is an ethics to preaching: I should not publicly talk in specifics about the lives of individuals I have observed or come to know. I have no right to do so. I certainly should not talk about myself. I am probably wrong about myself anyway—as the great psychologist Carl Jung used to say—and my story is not the same as the gospel of Jesus Christ. More: the sermon is not a partisan political speech or a tool of social organizing or even a news report. But I do mean that what I say about human need and God's mercy will have a context and ought to be recognizable as the truth. Manifest injustice, tragic news reports, and the needy earth itself cannot remain unmentioned: the gospel of God is spoken to this time; God's salvation and love are for this earth, now. But even more important is that the preacher have a sense of human sorrow and a delight in human joy, that the preacher see and care about the people among whom the sermon takes place. Such a care will not so much provide the content of a sermon as its tone.

> The word is our Lord Jesus Christ himself as the concretion in redemptive action of the love of the Creator for his creatures—and if the preaching of the word be not thus centered, it cannot avoid being swallowed up by categories of moral counsel and religious idealism.
> Joseph Sittler, *The Anguish of Preaching*[14]

Study of the texts is surrounded by attention and imagination. These provide materials for preaching, but they do not yet give us a sermon. How will the sermon actually be composed and then preached?

Composing the sermon and giving it

A final step in study is this: ask yourself how these texts give words and images for our need and God's mercy in Christ, for law and gospel. In answering this question, you will decide if the focus of the sermon will be on one of the texts, with the others as support, or on all three side by side. The other questions we have outlined will also help at this final stage: How do these texts give words for the death and resurrection of Jesus Christ, for his gift of the Spirit, for his presence in the assembly now? How does the word you will proclaim speak the meaning of baptism? How will we eat and drink in the holy communion the gospel you preach in the sermon? How can you, using these texts, speak the forgiveness of God to us now? Will what you are thinking you will preach awaken your hearers to trust in God with their lives? And will you give us help, then, to see how this very faith will be active in love, turned toward our needy neighbor and the needy and ravaged earth? Can you do this latter without making it sound as if we, once again, will be thereby trying to earn the love of God, but precisely because such love and service do indeed flow from and celebrate God's great mercy to us sinners?

When you have once again asked these questions as a culmination of your study, when you have done as much of this study as is possible for you, given all that is asked of you, then let it all go. Go for a walk. Read a book. Spend time with people you love. Take a break. If you have done careful study, if the texts have worked in your imagination and attention all week, when you come back the sermon outline will be there—or almost there.

Then compose the sermon. Take the authority of the gospel, the only authority we have, and make your outline or write your text. As you do this, the law-and-gospel structure will return as the greatest help to your writing.

You will need to decide if you will write out a text from which to read the sermon or if you will make notes that you will use in the pulpit. There are advantages and disadvantages to both. The sermon should be an oral event in the flow of a communal liturgy, an event that occurs at a specific time.

> Preaching is primarily oral proclamation. Through human words, God continues to form people, speaking judgment and hope.
> *Principles for Worship*[15]

It ought not be a lecture or a written exercise or words for the ages. Outside of this communal liturgy a sermon may not make much sense. But preachers who use full manuscripts can learn much of the manuscript so well that they can actually deliver the sermon in a way that does not seem like reading. And a fully written text does allow the preacher to use more carefully crafted language and to avoid stuttering as he or she searches for the right word. On the other hand, preachers who use notes—I myself use both sides of a 3- by 5-inch card, for example—can also include a few carefully thought-out phrases and can go over such phrases in the last hour or so before the service in which the sermon will be preached.

Two further notes about the content of the sermon you prepare. I do not recommend making up a story or a joke to begin with. That will call attention to you and make your approach to your real subject even more difficult. The imagery with which the Bible is full is itself strong enough. You can actually begin with one or more of the texts you have been given, not with something else. And do not add to the texts by trying to imagine what people felt like then, when the texts contain no such thing. Similarly, do not present the witness of the gospels as if they give accurate historical reports. Rather, it is wise for the preacher to honestly say that this is what Matthew or Mark says as they give witness to the meaning of Jesus Christ. When one speaks of what Jesus actually does, it should be what the risen Jesus is doing here, now.

In any case, when you are done, ask the questions we have asked again: The presence of Jesus Christ for this people? law and gospel? the cross? the Trinity? the sacraments? actually giving forgiveness? the turn to needy neighbor and needy earth? Are they here?

And then, once again, let it be. Pray and then let it be. In the morning, before preaching, give yourself another fifteen minutes to look at what you have prepared. Practice the opening sentences in your mind. Then go into the liturgy and trust that it is true when the assembly answers your greeting in the triune God with "And also with you." The Lord be in your heart and on your lips, dear preacher.

Then, here are five words of counsel for you in doing the preaching:

- Avoid "preacher's tone." Speak carefully and clearly but in your natural and honest voice. Follow George Herbert's counsel for dipping everything in your heart before you speak it. Let your honest words be "heart-deep," though not in maudlin pretense. Speak with both genuine authority and genuine humility. Be yourself: beloved of God, baptized, called to preach. And speak also to yourself, in both admonition and consolation.

He [the country parson] often tells them [his congregation] that sermons are dangerous

> things, that none goes out of church as he came in, but either better or worse; that none is careless before his judge, and that the word of God shall judge us. . . . But the character of his sermon is holiness; he is not witty, or learned, or eloquent, but holy. . . . [This] is gained . . . by dipping and seasoning all our words and sentences in our hearts, before they come into our mouths, truly affecting and cordially expressing all that we say; so that the auditors may plainly perceive that every word is heart-deep.
>
> George Herbert, *The Country Parson*[16]

- Honor the scripture you are proclaiming and honor the people in the assembly where you are preaching. Indeed, love those people, even when you are preaching the law. People are quite able to tell if the preacher actually despises them. When that begins to happen to a pastor, it is time for him or her to quit.

- Do not walk around. Stay near to the Bible or lectionary you are proclaiming. Be seen to be serving it. Stay in the ambo or pulpit, whatever is the liturgical "place of the word." Walking around only calls attention to yourself, as if you were exempted from the communal liturgical flow, as if you were more important than you are.

- Think about Sarah Morgan's experience of one nineteenth-century preacher. It is really true that bad preaching can make even the most wonderful biblical texts seem awful.

> A long, stupid sermon from that insufferable bore, Mr Garie, gave me a dreadful head ache. Does it not seem that the ministry is overstocked with fools? I grew perplexed and weary of his never ending stupidity, and assiduously read my hymnbook and would have learned it by heart, if his voice had not been so aggravating. . . . Invariably, the most beautiful passages of the Bible, those I cry over alone, appear absurd from his lips. I don't feel like a Christian. I shall not go hear him again.
> Sarah Morgan, *The Civil War Diary of a Southern Woman*[17]

- Preach Christ. Preach the cross. Actually speak the life-giving forgiveness of God now. And take joy in this vocation you have.

Then, when you are done, receive holy communion in the flow of the rest of the liturgy. Receive it for the forgiveness of your sins, including your sins in preaching. Give what you can and welcome the mercy of Christ. Do what you can, and then also forgive yourself.

A schedule for the Sunday preacher's week

So, here follows one idea. Dear preacher, it is only one idea. It may not work for you, and there may be weeks when all of its steps are not possible at all. Or it may sometimes be condensed into two hours of intense work. It is nonetheless set out here as a stimulus for your own thought and scheduling.

Sunday afternoon or Monday: Read the texts, in the order of gospel, then first reading, then second reading. You might outline each one, noting important phrases or images. Begin to think about them. Note difficult or puzzling passages. Pray.

Tuesday: Read the texts in Greek and Hebrew (or another language). Check words in a lexicon. Think about how the gospel text is different from parallel passages in the other gospels. Think about how the gospel text goes toward and already expresses the cross and resurrection of Jesus and the presence of the Risen One in the assembly today as that gospel book proclaims these things. Follow up on any intertextual references you discover, especially those in the gospel. Read the other texts in the context of the biblical book in which they occur. Make notes of anything you find in all this study.

Wednesday: Think about how the images of the first reading are reborn in the gospel. Write down one or two verbal images from the readings that you may want to use. Then read the commentaries and any preaching helps. Think again about difficult passages.

Also Wednesday, or another day: Take part in a text study group.

Thursday: Read all the other liturgical texts and hymns being used at the service for which you are preparing. Pay special attention to the prayer of the day, the hymn of the day, and the psalm.

Monday through Saturday: Do your ministry among your people; read a good newspaper; read a novel or another good book; go to the movies or stream a good film; keep thinking about your sermon; pray.

Friday: Ask yourself how these texts together may express our need and God's mercy, the cross, the sacraments, the Trinity, the presence of Jesus Christ now. You may find the "worksheet for sermon preparation" that follows a useful means for summarizing your study. In any case, using law and gospel, begin to make an outline.

Friday or Saturday: Take a walk or do something with people you love and with whom you relax or otherwise rest. Then take courage and compose your sermon.

Sunday: Preach the gospel of Jesus Christ in the assembly; receive communion yourself. Rest.

Sunday afternoon or Monday: Begin again.

> Then he began to say to them, "Today this scripture has been fulfilled in your hearing."
> Luke 4:21

> Then beginning with Moses and all the prophets, he interpreted to them the things about himself in all the scriptures. . . . They said to each other, "Were not our hearts burning within us while he was talking to us on the road, while he was opening the scriptures to us?"
>
> Luke 24:27, 32

A worksheet for sermon preparation

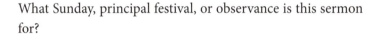

What Sunday, principal festival, or observance is this sermon for?

What are the lectionary texts?

What is the psalm? What antiphon does ELW suggest?

What is the hymn of the day? Quote a phrase from the hymn that might be helpful to you:

What themes are present in the prayer of the day?

What puzzle or difficulty is present in the texts and will not quickly resolve in your mind?

What is the situation of human need and sin, "the law," in the terms or images of the following?

>First reading:

>Second reading:

>Gospel:

What is the presence of grace in the crucified and risen Christ, "the gospel," in the terms or images of the following?

>First reading:

>Second reading:

>Gospel:

What is the relationship of the first reading to the gospel reading?

What other Old Testament references does the gospel reading make?

How does the second reading represent the gospel in the life of the church?

What does a commentary or a lectionary resource say that strikes you as helpful?

What is at least one thing that happened this week—in world events, in your community, in the natural world around you—that you find to be in important juxtaposition to the readings?

What commemorations occur near to the time of your preaching? Might they help with imaging what a life of faith looks like or how these texts might lead to faith active in love?

How do these texts express the meaning of the cross? the gift of the Spirit? the presence of the Trinity?

How might these texts express what is given to us in baptism?

How do they express what is given in holy communion?

List one to three images from the texts or from the liturgy that you hope to use in your sermon:

Summarize the thesis of your sermon in two sentences, law and gospel:

Conclusion

Consider again the image on the cover of this book. Painted by the Cranachs, who were painters and printers in Wittenberg, it shows Martin Luther preaching in the congregation of his university town. It also concretely shows the current communal task of the faithful preacher of the living Word.

Situated as it is in St. Mary's Church, right above the altar table of that congregation, the cross at the center of the image functions as this church's altar cross. The holy communion served from that table proclaims the cross, giving the assembly to eat and drink from the crucified Christ. At the same time, situated as it is between the imaged preacher and the congregation, the cross represents the very word of preaching present in the room, the word full of Christ's cross. But the blowing loincloth proposes that this Crucified One is also the Risen One, and from him flows the Spirit that through word and sacrament makes us alive together with him. Real people with real needs face both the cross and the preacher. The congregation spills beyond the margin of the painting to include more people—perhaps us, perhaps many others from all the needy world. The preacher opens the Bible or lectionary and on the grounds of its texts takes authority to preach the life and hope and forgiveness that are in the cross of Christ. The preacher (in this case, Luther) points not to himself but to the cross.

Everything is here: word and sacrament in an open assembly to which we also are drawn; the death and resurrection of Christ at the center; the preacher bringing this meeting around Christ to expression; the sermon as words full of Christ and the Spirit, spoken in juxtaposition to the holy communion and addressed in love to the assembly, that it may trust God.

Much joy to you, dear preacher of the church, in this very vocation.

End notes

[1] *Evangelical Lutheran Worship* (Minneapolis: Augsburg Fortress, 2006), 92.

[2] *The Use of the Means of Grace: A Statement on the Practice of Word and Sacrament* (Minneapolis: Evangelical Lutheran Church in America, 1997), Principle 1.

[3] Justin, 1 Apology, adapted from the translation of Gordon W. Lathrop, in *Holy Things: A Liturgical Theology* (Minneapolis: Fortress Press, 1993), 45.

[4] *Renewing Worship 2: Principles for Worship* (Minneapolis: Augsburg Fortress, 2002), Application P-4a, based on *The Use of the Means of Grace,* principle 34.

[5] *Constitution on the Sacred Liturgy* (Collegeville: Liturgical Press, 1963), 51.

[6] Martin Luther, "A Brief Instruction on What to Look for and Expect in the Gospels," in *Word and Faith,* ed. Kirsi I. Stjerna, vol. 2, *The Annotated Luther* (Minneapolis: Fortress Press, 2015), 32–33.

[7] *The Use of the Means of Grace,* application 9A.

[8] The Augsburg Confession, in *The Book of Concord,* ed.

Robert Kolb and Timothy J. Wengert, (Minneapolis: Fortress Press, 2000), 40.

[9] The Augsburg Confession, 41.

[10] The Augsburg Confession, 42.

[11] John Donne, *Poetry and Prose,* ed. Frank J. Warnke (New York: Random House, 1967), 345.

[12] James Baldwin, *Go Tell It on the Mountain* (New York: Dell, 1953), 204–5.

[13] *Renewing Worship 2: Principles for Worship* (Minneapolis: Augsburg Fortress, 2002), Principle P-13.

[14] Joseph Sittler, *The Anguish of Preaching* (Philadelphia: Fortress, 1966), 85.

[15] *Renewing Worship 2: Principles for Worship,* application P-5C.

[16] George Herbert, *The Country Parson, The Temple,* ed. John N. Wall Jr. (New York: Paulist, 1981), 62–63.

[17] Sarah Morgan, *The Civil War Diary of a Southern Woman* (New York: Simon & Schuster, 1991), 269.

Further reading for the preacher

Three classics

Luther, Martin. "A Brief Instruction on What to Look for and Expect in the Gospels." In *Word and Faith,* ed. Kirsi I. Stjerna, 28–37. Vol. 2 of *The Annotated Luther.* Minneapolis: Fortress Press, 2015.

Sittler, Joseph. *The Anguish of Preaching.* Philadelphia: Fortress Press, 1966.

Steumpfle, Herman G., Jr. *Preaching Law and Gospel.* Philadelphia: Fortress Press, 1978.

Three books on the Revised Common Lectionary

Graham, Fred Kimball, compiler. T*he Revised Common Lectionary: 20th Anniversary Annotated Edition.* Minneapolis: Fortress Press, 2012.

Ramshaw, Gail. *A Three-Year Banquet: The Lectionary for the Assembly.* Minneapolis: Augsburg Fortress, 2004.

———. *Treasures Old and New: Images in the Lectionary.* Minneapolis: Fortress Press, 2002.

Eight helpful books on homiletics

Buechner, Frederick. *Telling the Truth: The Gospel as Tragedy, Comedy, and Fairy Tale.* San Francisco: Harper & Row, 1977.

LaRue, Cleophus J. *I Believe I'll Testify: The Art of African American Preaching.* Louisville: Westminster John Knox, 2011.

Lord, Jennifer L. *Finding Language and Imagery: Words for Holy Speech.* Minneapolis: Fortress Press, 2010.

Mitman, F. Russell. *Preaching Adverbially.* Grand Rapids: Eerdmans, 2018.

Quivik, Melinda A. *Serving the Word: Preaching in Worship.* Minneapolis: Fortress Press, 2009.

Skudlarek, William. *The Word in Worship: Preaching in a Liturgical Context.* Nashville: Abingdon, 1981.

Willimon, William H. *Peculiar Speech: Preaching to the Baptized.* Grand Rapids: Eerdmans, 1992.

Wilson, Paul Scott. *The Four Pages of the Sermon: A Guide to Biblical Preaching.* Nashville: Abingdon, 1999.

A few collections of sermons and sermon helps

Sundays and Seasons. Published annually by Augsburg Fortress.

Sundays and Seasons: Preaching. Published annually by Augsburg Fortress.

Holmes, Stephen Mark, ed. *The Fathers on the Sunday Gospels.* Collegeville, MN: Liturgical Press, 2012.

Ramshaw, Gail, ed. *Richer Fare: Reflections on the Sunday Readings.* New York: Pueblo, 1990.

Toal, M. F., ed. *The Sunday Sermons of the Great Fathers,* 4 vols. Chicago: Regnery, 1958.

Further writing from the author on biblical preaching in the liturgy

Lathrop, Gordon W. "The Pastor in Preaching: Word." In *The Pastor: A Spirituality,* 41–58. Minneapolis: Fortress Press, 2006.

———. "Preaching, Eucharist, and Baptism according to the Gospel." In *The Four Gospels on Sunday: The New Testament and the Reform of Christian Worship,* 166–73. Minneapolis: Fortress Press, 2012.

———. "Word: Lectionary, Preaching, Hymnody." In *Saving Images: The Presence of the Bible in Christian Liturgy,* 123–44. Minneapolis: Fortress Press, 2017.

Other texts mentioned here

Baldwin, James. *Go Tell It on the Mountain.* New York: Dell, 1953.

Kolb, Robert, and Timothy J. Wengert, eds. *The Book of Concord: The Confessions of the Evangelical Lutheran Church.* Minneapolis: Fortress Press, 2000.

Constitution on the Sacred Liturgy. Collegeville, MN: Liturgical Press, 1963.

Donne, John. *Poetry and Prose.* Edited by Frank J. Warnke. New York: Random House, 1967.

Evangelical Lutheran Worship. Minneapolis: Augsburg Fortress, 2006.

Herbert, George. *The Country Parson, The Temple.* Edited by John N. Wall. New York: Paulist, 1981.

Morgan, Sarah. *The Civil War Diary of a Southern Woman.* New York: Simon & Schuster, 1991.

Mueller, Craig. *Indexes to Evangelical Lutheran Worship.* Minneapolis: Augsburg Fortress, 2007.

Principles for Worship. Minneapolis: Evangelical Lutheran Church in America, 2002.

The Use of the Means of Grace: A Statement on the Practice of Word and Sacrament. Minneapolis: Evangelical Lutheran Church in America, 1997.

Westermeyer, Paul. *Hymnal Companion to Evangelical Lutheran Worship.* Minneapolis: Augsburg Fortress, 2010